Dear Educator,

Thank you for purchasing "Gris y sus amigos." This book is the first in the series called *Los colores*.

The friendship journeys will introduce your emergent or beginner reader to Spanish through simple color theory and writing practice.

These hand-drawn workbooks are made to inspire your student and provide a shared learning experience that is as lovely as the pages themselves.

First, your student is introduced to primary and secondary color mixing theory as it relates to the color wheel (located in the back of the book). He/she can practice coloring in the primary and secondary colors in the wheel provided. Additionally, your student can see the color change in the fish themselves as they touch each other's fins.

Next, the student is introduced to the color words and other target vocabulary. Since writing is a superior way for your student to learn vocabulary and familiarize him/her with this phonetic language, target vocabulary is broken down into syllables on most of the story pages for your student to copy.

For example, the target word "rojo" will appear as :
ro-jo

___-___.   Your student writes <u>ro</u> - <u>jo.</u>

Additional vocabulary work and sound reinforcement is provided in the *Seño's Color Song* and in the *Syllable Work* worksheets. Both worksheets help to reinforce attention to detail and the *Syllable Work* worksheet, when completed, results in a lovely work of art.

To further personalize this workbook and enhance a feeling of ownership and attention to detail, encourage your student to color in the ocean and the sky with his or her color of choice. You can talk about the color choices and whether or not the color is primary or secondary.

If your student enjoys the finished workbook as his or her own work of art and would like to add more workbooks, then consider purchasing other workbooks in this series.

Please note that you can receive a copy of Seño's color song by contacting me at: mtvdoherty@gmail.com

Best wishes,

Mary Doherty
(creator of everybodyspanish.com)

Pronunciation note:

Please note that Spanish is a phonetic language, so what you see is what you get. To pronounce "a,e,i,o" sounds and their names, please refer to the pronunciation in the "Do, re, mi, fa" musical scale. The vowel "u" is always pronounced like the "u" in the word, "tutu."

The "j" is like an h. The "h" has no sound. The "v" is a cross between a "b" and a "v."

Rojo, Amarillo, y Azul
son amigos.
Ellos juegan juntos.

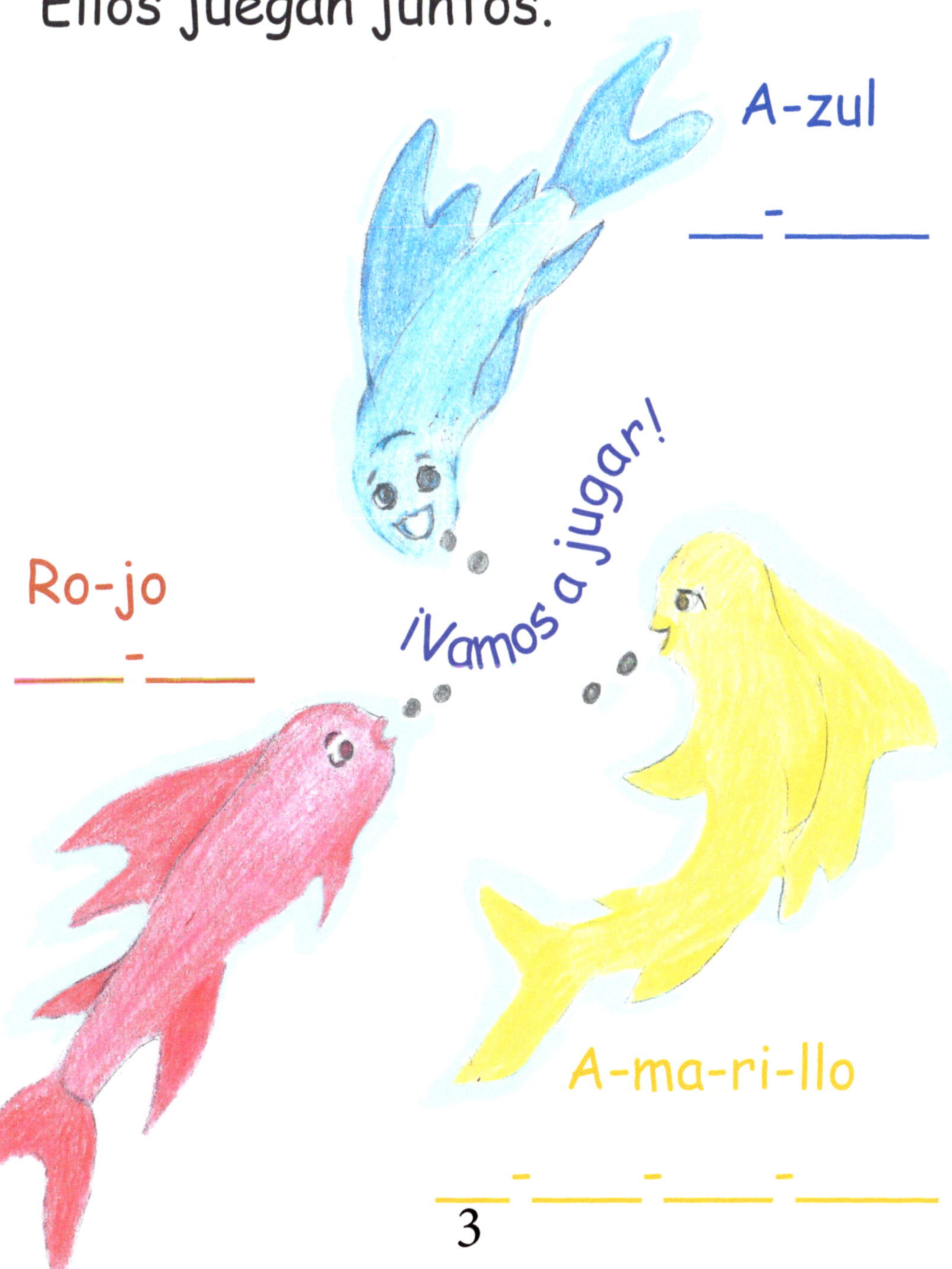

Cuando Rojo y Amarillo juegan
viene Anaranjado a jugar.

¿Puedo jugar?

A-na-ran-ja-do

_ _ _ _ _ _ _ _ _ _ _ _

Amarillo y azul dan verde.

Ver-de

____-__

Ahora, Morado quiere jugar.

♪ Deciden can-tar ...
____-____

Rojo, amarillo, azul, los primarios.
Rojo, amarillo, azul, los primarios.
Anaranjado, verde, morado, los secundarios.

Los colores del arco iris no tienen gris...

Mamá, quiero ser
otro color.
No me gusta el gris.

yo quiero lucir como ellos. Tú eres perfecto como eres.

¿ Pue-do ir ?

_ ____-_ ___ _

Sí, pero regresa pronto y te quiero.

____

¡Hola
Gris!

Los peces juegan
y juegan.

Ju-gar

___-___

12

Los peces empiezan a cantar...

"Rojo, amarillo, azul, los primarios...
anaranjado, verde, morado los secundarios"...

"No me gusta esa canción," dice Gris.

"¿Por qué, no?" preguntan los peces.

"Porque el arco iris no tiene gris
y me siento olvidado," dice Gris.

ar-co
___-___

i-ris
__-___

Rojo, Amarillo, y Azul
son amigos.
Ellos juegan juntos.

"¡Sí, Gris es importante!"

Los nubes son grises.

Los nubes grises traen la lluvia.

Son las gotitas de la lluvia

con la luz del sol

que producen

el arco iris.

"Pero, no soy un nube. Soy un pez.

¿Cómo importo yo?" pregunta Gris.

"¿Cómo importas tú?

Facil...

Tú reflejas todo.

Blan-co

_____-__

Tú vienes de Blanco y Negro.

Blanco no tiene color y negro

tiene todos los colores."

Ne-gro

___-___

16

¡Soy un acertijo!

¿Qué no tiene color y
tiene todos los colores
al mismo tiempo?

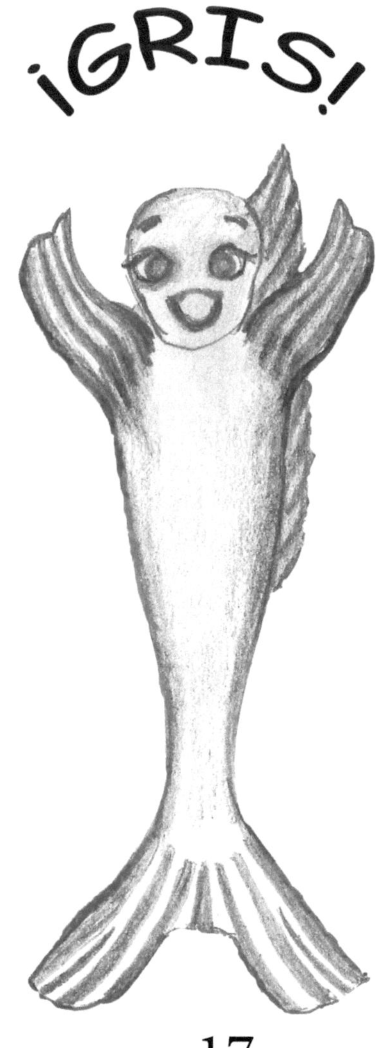

Page 1	
Rojo, Amarillo, y Azul son amigos.	Red, Yellow, and Blue, are friends.
Ellos juegan juntos.	They play together.
Vamos a jugar.	Let's play.
Page 2	
Amarillo y azul dan verde.	Yellow and blue make green.
Quiero jugar.	I want to play.
Page 3	
Cuando Rojo y Amarillo juegan viene Anaranjado a jugar.	When Red y Yellow play, Orange comes to play.
¿Puedo jugar?	Can I play?
Page 4	
Rojo y azul dan morado.	Red and blue make purple.
Ahora, Morado quiere jugar.	Now, Purple wants to play.
Page 5	
Deciden cantar.	They decide to sing.
Rojo, amarillo, azul, los primarios.	Red, yellow, blue, the primary colors.
Anaranjado, verde, morado, los secundarios.	Orange, green, purple, the secondary colors.
Page 6	
Los colores del arco iris no tienen gris.	The colors of the rainbow don't have grey.
Mamá, quiero ser otro color.	Mom, I want to be another color.
No me gusta el gris.	I don't like grey.
Page 7	
Yo quiero lucir como ellos.	I want to look like them.
Tú eres perfecto como eres.	You are perfect as you are.
Page 8	
¿Puedo ir?	Can I go?
¿Puedo jugar con ellos?	Can I play with them?

18

Sí, pero regresa pronto y te quiero.	Yes, but come back soon and I love you.
Page 9	
Hola gris.	Hi Grey.
Page 10	
Los peces juegan y juegan.	The fish play and play.
Page 11	
Los peces empiezan a cantar...	The fish begin to sing.
Rojo, amarillo, azul, los primarios...	Red, yellow, blue, the primary colors.
anaranjado, verde, morado los secundarios	orange, green, purple, the secondary colors.
No me gusta esa canción dice Gris.	I don't like that song says Grey.
ar-co i-ris	rainbow
Page 12	
Vamos todos.	Let's go everyone.
Hablar	to talk
Vamos todos hablar con el arco iris.	Let's go everyone to talk to the rainbow.
Page 13	
Sí, Gris es importante.	Yes, Grey is important.
Los nubes son grises.	The clouds are grey.
Los nubes grises traen la lluvia.	The grey clouds bring the rain.
Son las gotitas de la lluvia con la luz del sol que producen el arco iris.	They are the little drops of rain with the light of the sun that produce the rainbow.
Page 14	
Pero, no soy un nube.	But, I am not a cloud.
Soy un pez.	I am a fish.
¿Cómo importo yo? pregunta Gris.	How am I important? Grey asks.
¿Cómo importas tú?	How are yo important?
Facil	Easy
Tú reflejas todo.	You reflect all.

Tú vienes de Blanco y Negro.	You come from White and Black.
Blanco no tiene color y negro tiene todos los colores.	White has no color and black has all the colors.
Blanco	White
Negro	Black
Page 15	
Soy un acertijo.	I am a riddle.
Qué no tiene color y tiene todos los colores al mismo tiempo.	What doesn't have color and has all the colors at the same time.
Gris.	Grey

Seño's Color Wheel

La rueda de color

Los Primarios

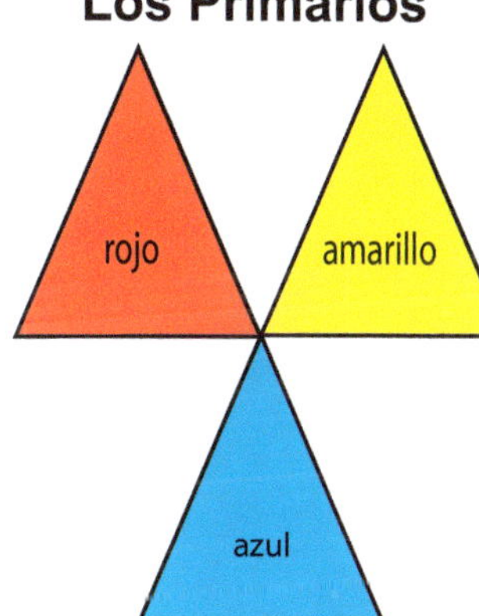

Los Secundarios

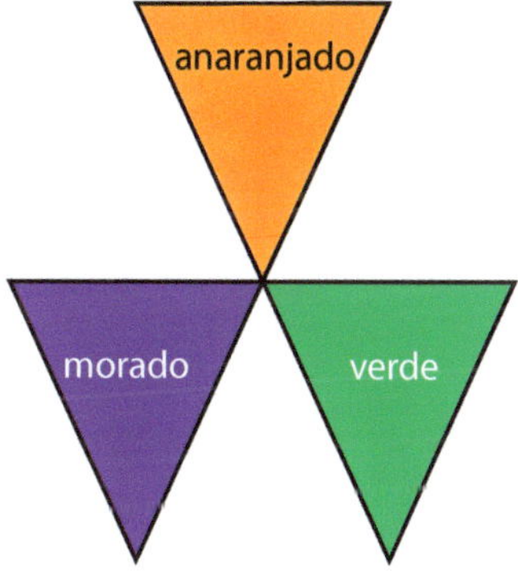

Color in your color wheel:

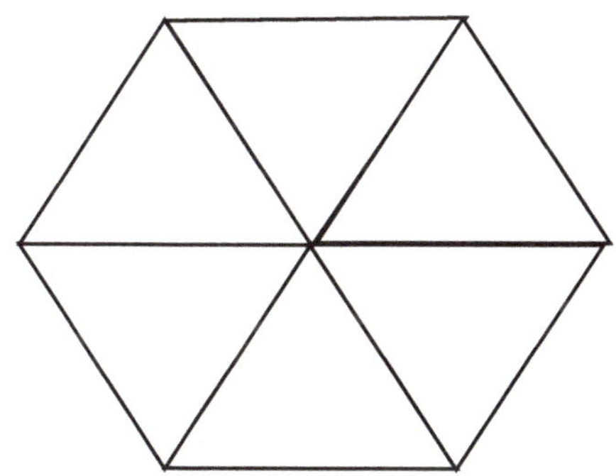

Seño's Colors Song

Rojo, amarillo, azul, los primarios

red, yellow, blue, the primaries

Rojo, amarillo, azul, los primarios

red, yellow, blue, the primaries

Anaranjado, verde, morado, los secundarios

orange, green, purple, the secondaries

Anaranjado, verde, morado, los secundarios

orange, green, purple, the secondaries

Los colores del arco iris no tienen gris

The colors of the rainbow don't have gray.

Los colores del arco iris no tienen gris

The colors of the rainbow don't have gray.

Gris viene de blanco y negro, gris

Gray comes from white and black, gray

written by: Mary Doherty (Seño)

Seño's Color Song worksheet

Fill in the ovals below with the corresponding color. Please notice the gray (gris), white (blanco), and black (negro) circles.

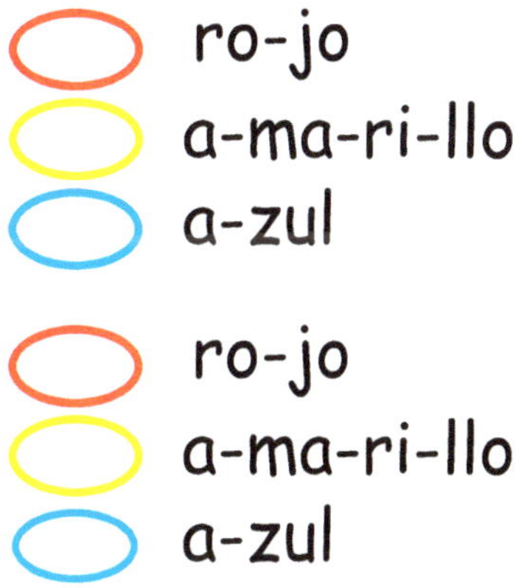

ro-jo
a-ma-ri-llo
a-zul

ro-jo
a-ma-ri-llo
a-zul

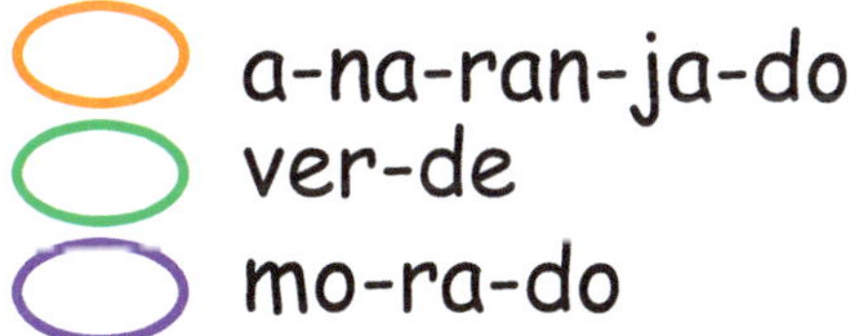

a-na-ran-ja-do
ver-de
mo-ra-do

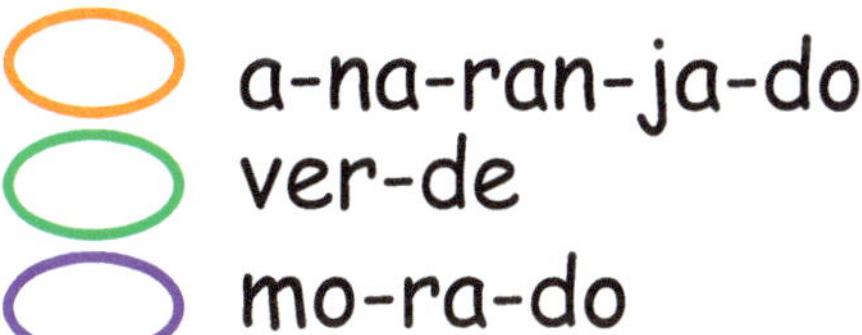

a-na-ran-ja-do
ver-de
mo-ra-do

Los colores del arco iris no tienen gris ◯
Los colores del arco iris no tienen gris ◯
Gris ◯ viene de blanco ◌ y negro ◯
Gris ◯

Syllable Work

ro-jo   a-na-ran-ja-do   los co-lo-res
a-ma-ri-llo   ver-de   del ar-co i-ris
a-zul   mo-ra-do   no tie-nen gris

Gris vie-ne de blan-co y ne-gro

de	tie	ran	ris	res
vie	ro	ar	gro	na
a	ne	jo	do	nen
co	llo	ne	a	i
Gris	los	ri	ver	blan
ma	do	co	de	mo
del	y	gris	zul	lo
ja	no	ra	co	a

Continue coloring in the syllables with the appropriate color and chose you own colors or patterns for non-color words.